BENT MIND

POETRY TO TEASE THE MIND, ENGAGE THE HEART, FREE THE SPIRIT

M.R. LENNON

M.R. LENNON

IN MEMORY OF
JOYCE LENNON
1982

INTRODUCTION

This small book, I hope, will spur thoughts on your view of matters. Little twists, turns, and plays on words that the mind will dwell on. With storytellers, yes, that is you the reader too, our stories come from life. In these pages, I have collected some of mine about actual people, experiences, and thoughts I have pondered, or you may say blundered through, in my life. I have included the award-winning poem "The Clear Pane of It" for your reading pleasure. I hope you will enjoy my take on a few matters.

CONTENTS

MIND BENDING

POEMS THAT WILL CONTORT THE MIND

I am Man

Madness, fear, confusion I sow
I give no illusion of who, or what, I am
For I am not the harbinger of discord,
I am discord
Smoke and mirrors is my intention
Those steps of elusion hide not from me
For I sew knots of dissension in their hearts
Fighting amongst themselves is all I wish
For I am happy with the allusion I have given
They say I have brought the world chaos
Yes, yes I have
I am all that is chaos
I am Chaos
I am Man

The Clear Pane of It

They see through me, but they do not see me
Here I am, clear as crystal, but they see me not
My existence invisible to them, but I am here
Not seen through the pane, a pence I need
Daily they pass, looking through my pane
They see me not, but they will with time
For my grime comes with time
They see my grime, but not me
To rid the grime they see, rids me
So they rid the grime, withholding the pence
They see me not, through my pane
Can you see me?
Can you really?
My pain is crystal clear

Seek it Today

Seek it today, not tomorrow
For knowledge is relevant today
For tomorrow's history is today
So seek knowledge today

If knowledge is not sought today
Tomorrow shall lack history
Tomorrow's history today
Shall be absent

Unsought knowledge of today
Lost to tomorrow's history
For tomorrow will never be today
What of tomorrow?

To wait till tomorrow
Today will be lost
Knowledge is for today
Not to be lost on tomorrow

Waiting for tomorrow
Shall make dust of you
So, my friend
Seek knowledge today

For tomorrow never comes

Mistress of the Edge

Heart pounding, mind racing, anxiety raging
Are you insane? Oh God, the pain!
That's where she lurks, that point of uncertainty
The edge of insanity
Caressing your fear
Friend? Foe? You'll never know
Oh, but she wants you so
At the Void's edge
Just a little closer, what could it hurt?
Sane? Insane? She brings much psychogenic pain
Always she is there, haunting the irrational ledge
She will show you the deranged edge of reality
Love her? Fear her? Hate her?
You will embrace her

Embittered

Is it fair?
I say, depart
Take thy snare
Thou not entangle my heart

Sharp is thy tongue
Bitter in thy soul
Thou reek of dung
For I pay thy toll

Agitation thy gift to me
Acrid is the mood
For thou bring tomfoolery
I shall hasten thy tomb

A subtle piercing edge
Thou might plea to me
Release I shall pledge
To set thou free

Rejoice in my heart
Freedom from thy snare
Upon thy depart
It is fair!

Lines may also be read from bottom to top

For the Whole Sake of Nothing

An empty place I am
For that is what I am told
Filled with nothing
But I am something

This is confusing, I must say
Missing is all of me
But I am complete
Empty of all, missing nothing

If there were something at the heart of me
I would not be
To be nothing, is to be me
Something empty of all

Sorry that I am empty and missing nothing
But you understand
I must be a hole lot of nothing
To be all I am

The Toll of the Soul

Clank Clank Clank
The defiled bell tolls

Clank Clank Clank
Time will unfold

Clank Clank Clank
The soul dies ninefold

Clank Clank Clank
Lost is the soul to the hole

Secret of the Known

Of known, **What** is known?
Nothing, if **You** seek not
You may **Think** you know
Knowledge forsakes **You,** through arrogance
The arrogant should **Know,** the seeker's humility
To seek **Is** to want
He who wants **Not,** shall find not
Ignorance is **What** they find
I pray **You** shall seek
The humble **Need** of knowledge
For ignorance **To** be overcome
You must **Know** the known

— . —

HEART SPRING

A SPRING WELLING WITH HEART FELT POEMS

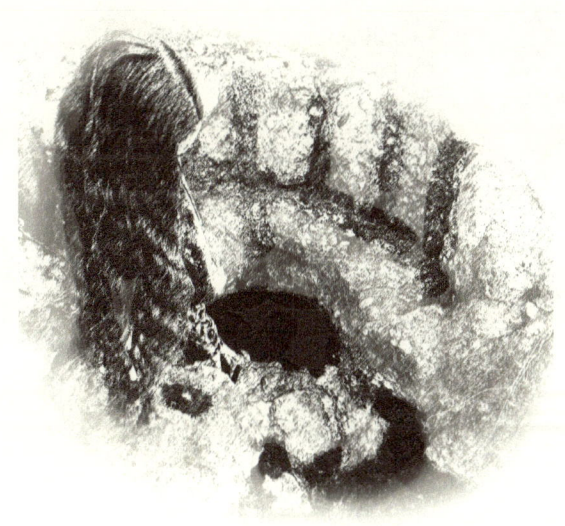

Chill

Chill embraces me
Claws dig deep
Lustfully drawing on me

As I walk the wood
She will not release me
Hindering my progress
She knows my path

Chill wants me, my heat
I feel her claws deep
Deep with cold sleep
To my bones, she tears

Her anger rages
My path is true
Her jealousy has an icy heart
A heart that is not for me

My burden slows me
My path is true
Chill screams in my face
Frosty is her breath

My heart, I see her
My heart stands
A smile of love
Brow of concern
Eyes of want and warmth

Chill screams at her
Cold jealous rage
Frigid hatred for her

My purpose within sight
My burden pulling down
Chill laughing with glee
Claws deeper

Chill holds me not
My warmth is not my own
But of my Queen
A Dragon's fire
Is kindled by his Mystic's love

Chill screams with rage
She cannot have me
Heart of fire
Chill will never have

Only a Mystical Queen
May hold the burning heart of a Dragon

Chill, my heart is not yours
Leave me be

With luck

A hug, just one if you're lucky
Will change your life
All she is within one embrace
But guards them close
Not freely given to just any
Are you that lucky?

A kiss, just one will cost you
The price, heavy if you're lucky
For you must give your heart fully
That price she will accept only
For you to glimpse the love within her
That price, will you pay?
Do you feel lucky?

The Cuddle

To cuddle? Or not to cuddle?
You ask that question of me
It is not a question
It is an absurdity

It is absurd not to cuddle
What shall you do with your time?
That time with your love
Will you just sit on your hands?

Sitting on hands is unwise
For hands are meant to hold
To hold one's love true
To be unwise, leaves you unloved

Be the wise one, my friend
For arms, legs, hands, feet, fingers, and toes
Are for the cuddle of one's love true
Embrace the one you love with them all

For the cuddle is to love
So, to rid you of your question
To cuddle? Or not to cuddle?
I answer with wisdom: love, my friend, and cuddle

Her

For her eyes to fall upon you
Shall bring you to quiver
For her to take interest
Shall bring worth
For her to touch you
Shall bring freedom
For her to embrace you
Shall erase all sorrow
For her to love you
Shall bring life eternal

To Love a Woman

To love a woman
Is to know she is free
Enjoy her freedom

To love a woman
Is to protect her from the world
Give her the world

To love a woman
Is to know she will love you
Embrace her love

To love a woman
Is to be proud of her
Lose your pride

To love a woman
Is to know she needs held
Truly hold her

To love a woman
Is to know she wants your all
Be her all

To love a woman
Is to gain eternal joy

You Need One

Everyone needs one
A person cannot live without one
But very few have one
Do they not live?

To have one is to have all
All is lost without one
One shall find they're lost
To hold one is to be found

So be true of heart to one
Honor the one when found
Hold one close so you are not lost
Care for one, for one will care for you

Live for one true, for One is your life

Free Spirit

Poems of nomadic spirit

Horizon

Is that the horizon I see?
Her freedom teases me so
For the chase is what she wants of me
What do you think? Should I go?

Her timeless travels call to me
How far do you think I should go?
As far as my eyes can see?
Or farther than the flight of a crow?

Endless is her wander
Her spirit free from all
It makes me stop and ponder
Shall I go before the fall?

I must tell you, mate
Before society knows
Horizon is my date
And now, I must go!

Nomadic Soul

The time has come
I must admit, the truth of it
Facts tell true of anarchy's drum
Stepping out, I must commit

I see adventure at its core
Finding peace for my soul
Life's path to explore
Stepping out is my goal

Overcome freedom's fear
Anxiety held, one step will tell
Social exemption all too near
Stepping out, will ring that bell

I tell you so, that I must go
To seek immunity for my soul
Social chains shall be my foe
Stepping out is a nomad's role

A nomad's heart is true
For they have no doubt
Of the unshackled taboo
Of stepping out

The Flow

There they go
Away with the flow
No need to row
Go with the flow!

There, the defiant ones
Against the flow they row
Individualists cheer
"Go against the flow!"

I see them stress
Those who ride the flows
Maintaining success
While status grows

I see them writhe
The defiant ones
Fists raised high
Swimming against the flow

This river of life
With all its trappings
Eternal strife
An annoying yapping

Why must I choose
This way of life
Clearly a social ruse
Freedom is my wife

I may be a bore
This river not for me
I will stay ashore
To rid chaos with glee

If you seek what is true,
You tire of the flow,
Come, enjoy a mountain view
Let your freedom grow

Leave that river's flow
Free your heart and soul
Let chaos be your foe
Freedom is your goal

The Wander

In the wander I thrive
Endless ocean into I dive
For the journey keeps me alive

The wanderlust is deep in branding
I shall never find a home of landing
Thus, I maintain my nomadic standing

Not as patient as a frog
Or sedentary as a log
I shall eat adventure like a hog

Knowing my potential
With wandering so essential
I see society inconsequential

I cannot ignore the attitude of Saturn
I must pay heed to my nomadic yearn
In my wanders, I may not return

The Lost

May I ask
Are you lost?
Is life such a task?
If so, give it a toss!

To be lost
Is to be free
Never to regret the cost
That is the key

To be lost, is to live
Do not ponder
These words I give
Get lost! And wander!

The world is out there
Free to wander
Get out of your chair
And stop the ponder

You hold the key
There is no cost
Be free!
Become the lost!

Not My World

I choose to disagree
With this society
Not bow or bend a knee
For I seek autonomy

ACKNOWLEDGMENTS

To my heroes, my father and brother, always there for me. To my children, all grown up, love you beyond what you can imagine. Toni, an anarchist in the true sense of the word, these few pages would not be without your inspiration. Love you, Mystic. Dee, fabulous author of the fantasy realm, thank you for agreeing to proofread this bit of work. Wayne with Pure Impact Studios image editing, thanks, man. To you, the reader out there in the world, thank you.

THE AUTHOR

M.R. Lennon is a nomadic renunciate who meanders the country in his big green bus named Hermes. He is a glutton for knowledge; his mind hoards an infinite stock of useless facts. When he is not writing, you can find M.R. Lennon learning, exploring, and adventuring. He also works in mechanical design and as a handyman. M.R. Lennon is known for his mind-contorting style and passion for freedom.